Confessions of a Hopeless Romantic

Laura Smith

BookLeaf Publishing

Presentation by *BookLeaf Publishing*

Web: www.bookleafpub.com

E-mail: info@bookleafpub.com

ISBN : 9789357699693

First edition 2022

DEDICATION

Thank you for sharing so much love and so many beautiful memories with me, T. Most of all, thank you for inspiring me.

To everyone I have ever loved.

ACKNOWLEDGEMENT

To my family; thank you for your continued support and love I have been blessed with by you.

To my gorgeous little sister; thank you for being a part of my life and always helping me be kind to myself.

To my dearest friends Jason and Noor; thank you for being with me in my sadness, for sitting with me in my discontent and making so many beautiful memories in our happiness.

To BookLeaf Publishing; thank you for this amazing opportunity!

PREFACE

"We've all been there. Through the sleepless nights and ceaseless self-doubt and criticism. We've all been through the ups and downs, through the breakups and the heartbreaks, the highs and lows of life and relationships and what it means to exist in this world.

This book is a love letter to those experiences. Whether they were pleasant or uncomfortable, all elements of life deserve to be celebrated. They are, after all, what makes life itself."

This anthology of poems was born from a period of immense growth and change. The 21 poems contained between these covers are not confined by one theme; they embrace natural imagery, embody a desire to savour the small moments, and explore love through a lens of existentialism.

The second section of this anthology (from Poem 8 onwards) detail the inner thoughts and feelings during this period of metamorphosis; the end of my first relationship.

I hope that you can resonate with this anthology and find some peace and contentment within these pages.

Night time

The white light in an
otherwise dark azure
blossoms and wanes.
The pearly coin flips
over and over
falling and rising only
to fall and rise again.

The worlds billboard
boasts craters of us;
impressions left by ants
that crawled upon its surface
in their search for cheese.

That lone figure in the speckled sky
and I
have much in common.

I often look up to her and
Wonder
if you are watching her,
too.

Unspoken Words

Moving through life I find myself bending to
meet others will,
forever tending to their wounds before I consider
my own.
I adapt myself to suit their needs, alter parts of
me
to appease their demands
so that they can live carefree,
unburdened by the otherwise burden
of me.

Why do I do this?
What was it that made me mould myself into
the casts of others?
To melt each atom of my being to create one
more like theirs?
To scold myself for having needs and wants
and to long for a life like the one that I actually
want
to live

I am no longer content to sit idly by
and watch me betray my own essence.
I choose to tune out the demand ingrained in the
core of me
that says it isn't enough unless I give more;

It's not enough unless I devote
my life, my soul, my corpse
to the service of others.

I am deconstructing the origami
of my being,
pulling myself apart piece by
paper thin piece.
Unfurling the folds and smoothing
the wrinkles
forged from holding onto
a form that isn't mine
for far too long.

Love is

everywhere everywhere

Laughter peeling off of trees
As children play in the park

everywhere everywhere

Shy glances and hesitant hands
As teenagers hold them for the first time

everywhere everywhere

Hooded gazes and questioning brows
As hungry hands grasp for a taste of skin

everywhere everywhere

Warmth and light beaming from exhausted smiles
As mothers' welcome new life into the world

everywhere everywhere

Unconditional kindness and unwavering affection

As parents witness their babies becoming
parents

everywhere everywhere

Love is
Everywhere, everywhere.

Newly Discovered Forgotten Things

Eons of myself pass
in the beat of an eye
and whatever profound wisdom
or unearthed Universal truth
just discovered
is unremembered

How many artefacts of importance
from civilisations long past
lie buried within my body?
As millennia of myself proceed
their fleeting presence on my consciousness
a mayfly of inspiration

I launch myself after them.
Wind trying to catch smoke,
leaf clinging to a raindrop
as the blade bends
and the bead's miniscule weight
hauls itself   away

only to find my air clear
and my skin dry.

Spring Gardening

Mud and earth churn underneath me
as I rupture its surface with iron tools.
The dirt at the bottom of my garden
could use some life.

Tilling through the soft silt and muck
made muckier by recent storms
my shovel hits something hard
with a resounding *clunk*

Expecting a stone or jagged fragment of brick
from a time long ago,
Long before it ceased to be a wall,
I dig on
Scraping at the soil around my still-earthed
treasure.

What if it's a relic from the past?
Some precious artifact of silver or gold
unmarred by the changing seasons
and priceless to some exotic collector.

Or what if its a bone of something or someone
Long lost to this world?
What if some poor soul came to rest in my
backyard?

This garden is a living mortuary,
The resting place of someone in eternal rest.

Perhaps it's a door to another world?
A steel lid sealing shut an entire civilisation.
They could be small,
Using teaspoons as ladles and bottle caps as umbrellas.
Or are there giants lurking in caves beneath our homes?
A network of excavated rooms in the damp dinge of underground.

The handle's rust imprints itself
in my palms
as my grip tightens and
I keep digging.

650cc

The buzz in my ears
Keeps ringing
A hangover from
Time spent
Sat ontop of an
Engine
Going 110 miles
An hour

Whipping round corners
Blazing through streets
The sting of wind
On my face
A delightful pain
A symptom of speed
A caution of danger

"Go faster", I say

The Docks

Smears of incandescent oil
at the edge of the horizon
Shimmer so beautifully
in dusk light,
Smudging the sky with
rainbow hues

The gentle ebb and flow
of water loitering
below us;
A liquid ambience

Nearby ships and
faraway structures etch
the profile of the skyline
Detailing the edge of what
little my eyes can see
It looks little
from here, at least

You lean over the barrier
and see

The Remembering

A long glint of light rests on my bedsheets
one stray hair from a lover long past

I haven't changed them since you slept here
It sits there, all brown oak and red tinge

A crack on the surface of my reality

Delayed Change

The leaves of our love had long yellowed, but
We
painted ourselves green
and laughed as We watched
the seasons change around us.

We were reptiles clinging to our shed skin
hoping that the armour of
our past could protect us
from the agonising emergence of new flesh.

Our love was chalk
eroding itself through its expression
as swirling professions of fated love
sprawled their radiance over dull concrete

We thought that We were mightier than the
storm billowing around us,
that our affection was robust enough to
withstand the quakes that shuddered our earth
We only noticed the chasm between us when

/ we had already plummeted to it's depths /

Nothing 'bout this cold air feels like home

I lay in the ceramic cloud upon which my spirit
floats away
This white crucible of hot broth
This open coffin at sea
The heaviness resting over my body
a blanket against the crisp air of the world;
of the bitter truth of our worlds
now

Is there suddenly more steam in here?
Or is there more liquid in my eyes
to refract the whisps
in the candlelight?
We are Universes apart

but the love still feels as close

A cool pearl of liquid makes it's way
down my face
from the crease between my brows
down my nose and over the apple of my cheek
I can't tell if it's from the shower head or me
or both

Turn the music off

it's too loud within my soul tonight

It's easier to write when you're Sad

We are more open to revelations of truth
when we are burdened by uncomfortable
emotions.
How many great poets lived happy lives?
How many eminent songwriters were
unburdened by heartbreak and pain and loss?
If wisdom was born from happiness
then babies
or puppies
would be the sages and prophets of all time.

Futile

We were loving in vain
Trying to make just that enough
To disguise the problems and dillemas
Central to the fact that we simply
Don't belong together.
We didn't fit in ways that we need to,
Like two wrong sized planks of wood trying to make a bench
And crumbling under the weight of pigeons.

Escapism

I wish I could suffocate myself
in your imari fantasy
To submerge myself
so entirely
in memories of what it was like
to be yours
that I cease to be here
Now

If only anguish was a time machine
to execute my longing

laying in bed doing nothing

apathy
descends
upon my body
as dense fog rolls in from the hills
sudden and heavy
shrouding my energy in its entirety

lethargy
seeps
through my bones
the cloying, sticky heaviness presses down
on my arms and legs
and feet
and hands

sickness
rises
within me
that nauseous feeling of weight in your sinuses
and stomach;
the heaviness at the back of your throat

i would open a window
to get some fresh air
if i could move
or if i really cared to

Stop clenching your jaw

My muscles are sore from swirling
this sorrow around on my tongue
My mandible aches
from chewing this overcooked
steak over and over,
Each grind of my teeth
doesn't make it anymore tender
or any easier to consume

The process of Art

Poetry is like arts and crafts
with fragments of yourself.
You cut off a finger to examine it,
slowly turn it around in view,
get out the glue stick or cello tape
and find a suitable place on the page
to stick it to.

You can smother it in glitter all you want,
bathe it in superfluous adjectives and silentless
words
to dress up the gory details.
To make your product somewhat more palatable
to an audience.

But your end result remains just that -
a severed finger on the canvas.

Love / Alone

Love alone can't fill the void in conversation
as the silence hangs like a wilting vine
that bends in the breeze of its final breath
and your understanding fails to be understood.

Our love was the crooked salesman
who sold us a fairy tale of what we could be.
We were too busy dwelling on the laugher and
happiness
to notice the disconnect in our circuitry.

We built a magnificent castle on the ocean
and still wondered why our dinner tasted of wet
salt.

We wondered why we couldn't see each other
clearly
when we were already submerged
deep
within our own lack of foresight.
When we had seen each other as we were
knowing that we both wanted different.

O' ladle of my heart, shiny spatula of my eye,
I tried to love you enough to make you fit snug
within the confines of my kitchen drawers

and blamed you for jamming them
when you didn't.

I saw you for all that you were
and I love you for everything that you are,
but I still wanted love to be enough to make it
work.

Floating away

I am but a pebble
drifting away on the waves.
Though stormy waters churn the oceans around
me
the pounding spray on my porous form
will wash away the dents and cracks
marred on my surface by existence.

I'm still rough and jagged at the moment
But someday, I will be smooth.

The flowers you brought me for Valentine's Day

Their beauty has long been drained from them
as they sat
stoically on the windowsill,
watching the world move on
below their static bodies.
They saw the sun rise
and fall

only to watch the moon rise
and fall
only to see the sun ascend once more.
Waiting patiently as their life
returned to the very atmosphere that
first birthed it.

The bunch of flowers brought
over a month ago
are now as old as the flame who bought them.
Their vibrant, voluminous foliage
has shrunk,
shrivelled,
to less than half
the size of its former glory.

In the midst

of the sea of hollow brown
lifelessness,
there is one stalk of green.
The pink of its petals still visible
as it clings to the echoes of its life.

By all laws of nature, the puffy peach blush
of its frond
should have been long lost
to Time
as he mercilessly marches on.
They haven't had water since we ended things.

Isn't it a miracle
that death didn't mar the life of it?

The Next Love

My soul deserves a slow love.
A gentle desire that blossoms like a great oak.

The radiance of fiery passion more a glowing ember in the centre of us
smouldering its subtle heat, unperturbed by wind or cold.

I want the fall to be a glide as I savour the views on the way down.
I can close my eyes knowing that I will meet the ground softly.

Happy Endings

As the earth turns
the ending of each day
secures the beginning
of the next.
Tides of darkness
sweep across each hemisphere
to pave the way for
waves of light.

As the very sun
sets
it illuminates
the rainbow at the
edge of the world;
Decorating the sky
in vibrant hues of
tangerine and pink,
tingeing otherwise colourless clouds.

The seasons chase each other
through the years,
all leaving space for the others,
as the natural tick of each day
tocks on.
Sweet decay of organic matter
feeds our crops and nurtures

the growth of tomorrow.

In this beautiful cycle of being,
this dance of push and pull,
Death makes way for Life
just as Life makes way for Death.

www.ingramcontent.com/pod-product-compliance
Lightning Source LLC
Chambersburg PA
CBHW051750130826
49812CB00033B/1080
9789357699693